Calgary Flames

FOPLA / AABPO

Written by
Don Cruickshank

Published by Weigl Educational Publishers Limited
6325 – 10 Street SE
Calgary, Alberta, Canada
T2H 2Z9

Web site: www.weigl.com

Library and Archives Canada Cataloguing in Publication

Cruickshank, Don
        Calgary Flames / Don Cruickshank.

(Hockey in Canada)
Includes index.
ISBN 1-55388-258-X (bound)
ISBN 1-55388-259-8 (pbk.)

        1. Calgary Flames (Hockey team)--Juvenile literature.
I. Title. II. Series.

GV848.C28C78 2006   j796.962'6409712338   C2006-902125-2

Printed in the United States of America
1 2 3 4 5 6 7 8 9 0 10 09 08 07 06

We gratefully acknowledge the financial support of the Government of Canada through the Book Publishing Industry Development Program (BPIDP) for our publishing activities.

Editor
Frances Purslow

Design and Layout
Terry Paulhus

Contents

PAGE 6

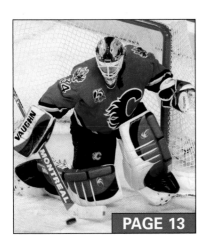

PAGE 13

PAGE 22

The History of the NHL

Hockey has been around for many years. Most historians credit James Creighton, a Canadian, with writing the first set of rules for hockey. These rules, called the Halifax Rules, are in the **Hockey Hall of Fame** in Toronto. In 1875, Creighton organized and played in the first official game of ice hockey using these rules. It was played at the Victoria Skating Rink in Montreal. About 18 years later, teams from the **Amateur** Hockey Association of Canada began competing for the **Stanley Cup**, called the Dominion Hockey Challenge Cup at the time. In 1914, the Stanley Cup became the exclusive trophy of two **professional** leagues. These leagues were the National Hockey Association (NHA) and the Pacific Coast Hockey Association (PCHA).

Three years later, the National Hockey League (NHL) was formed out of the NHA. The teams playing in the league at that time were the Montreal Canadiens, the Montreal Wanderers, the Toronto Arenas, and the Ottawa Senators.

The Stanley Cup was donated by Lord Stanley, who was governor general of Canada from 1888 to 1893.

ver the next 25 years, several other
ams joined and left the NHL. When the
reat Depression occurred in the 1930s,
e Montreal Maroons, the New York
mericans, and the original Ottawa
nators withdrew from the league due to
lack of **funds**. The remaining six teams
 the league at the start of the 1942–43
ason became known as the Original Six.
or the next 25 years, no new teams were
lowed into the league, and none of the
x teams changed locations. In 1967,
e NHL expanded by adding six new
anchises. Since that time, the league
s expanded many times.

oday, there are 30 teams in the NHL.
x are based in Canadian cities, and
e other 24 are in the United States.
he Canadian NHL teams are the
ancouver Canucks, the Edmonton
ilers, the Calgary Flames, the Toronto
aple Leafs, the Montreal Canadiens,
d the Ottawa Senators.

THE ORIGINAL SIX

Between the 1942–43 season and the
league's expansion in 1967, there were only
six teams in the NHL. They were the
Montreal Canadiens, the Toronto Maple
Leafs, the Detroit Red Wings, the Chicago
Blackhawks, the New York Rangers, and
the Boston Bruins. They are known as the
Original Six.

CHANGES THROUGHOUT THE YEARS

PAST	The puck was wooden.	There were seven players per team on the ice.	Forward passes were against the rules.	There were goal posts, but no nets. Goals were scored from either side of the goal line.
PRESENT	The puck is rubber.	There are six players per team on the ice.	Forward passes are allowed.	Nets are used.

The Rise of the Calgary Flames

1972

The Flames franchise joins the NHL. Their home town is Atlanta, Georgia. Their emblem is a fiery A. During the **Civil War**, much of the city of Atlanta burned to the ground. The Flames are named after this event.

1980

The Atlanta Flames move to Calgary. They keep their name and change their emblem to a fiery C. The Calgary Flames play their first NHL game. It is against the Quebec Nordiques, a team that has since moved to Denver and is now called Colorado Avalanche. The game ends in a 5–5 tie.

1986

The Flames defeat the Edmonton Oilers for the first time in a **playoff** series. They advance to the Stanley Cup finals but lose to the Canadiens in five games.

1989

The Flames win their first Stanley Cup. They defeat the Montreal Canadiens in six games. They become the first **opposition** team in the history of the NHL to win the Stanley Cup in the Montreal Forum. Flames fans are delighted.

1990

The Flames finish the regular season in second place in the Smythe Division, with 100 points. During playoffs, they lose a disappointing series to the Edmonton Oilers in game seven in overtime.

1992

The Flames miss the playoffs just two years after finishing the regular season as the league's best team. This is a difficult year for the Flames and their fans.

6

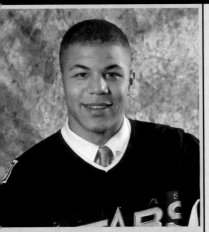

2004

The Flames make it all the way to the Stanley Cup finals. They lose to Tampa Bay Lightning in game seven of a thrilling series. They become the first Canadian team since the Vancouver Canucks in 1994 to play in the Stanley Cup finals.

995

Flames superstar, Jarome Iginla, is drafted in the first round of the NHL **Entry Draft** by the Dallas Stars. The Flames gain Iginla and Corey Millen in late 1995 in a trade for Joe Nieuwendyk. Iginla later develops into one of the league's best goal scorers.

1996–2003

The Flames miss the playoffs for seven years in a row. Fans in Calgary grow tired of their losing hockey team.

2002

The Flames hire Darryl Sutter as their new head coach and general manager. The team begins to win again under Sutter's guidance. They draft Dion Phaneuf from the Red Deer Rebels, a top young defenceman in the Canadian Hockey League, in the first round of the NHL Entry Draft.

2006

The Flames are defeated by the Anaheim Mighty Ducks in game seven of the first round of the playoffs.

Quick Facts

- Calgary is Canada's energy capital. Many oil and gas producers are based here.
- Calgary is Canada's fastest growing city.
- Calgary is known for its sunny skies and chinook winds, which can raise temperatures more than 20° Celsius in just a few hours.
- The Calgary Stampede is a 10-day rodeo that occurs in July. It attracts more than a million visitors to the city each year.
- Calgary's nickname is "Cow Town" because of its western roots. There are still many cattle ranches in the Calgary area.

Home of the Flames

The first home arena for the Flames was the Omni in Atlanta. When the Flames moved to Calgary in 1980, their home arena was the Stampede Corral. The Corral was built in 1950 for the Calgary Stampeders hockey club. The arena was small. It could only seat 7,242 fans.

Since then, the Corral has hosted Flames games, horse shows, boxing and wrestling matches, religious gatherings, and celebrity concerts. The Flames played three seasons in the Corral. In 1983, they played their last game in the Corral against the Edmonton Oilers. They won 6–5.

The Corral still hosts many events in Calgary. One of its busiest times each year is during the Calgary Stampede.

In 1983, the Flames moved into the Olympic Saddledome. The Saddledome was built for the 1988 Winter Olympic Games. Its pillar-free construction allows everyone to have a good view of events that occur in the building. Today, this world-class building is called the Pengrowth Saddledome. It has a seating capacity of more than 17,000.

■ The Pengrowth Saddledome has one of the largest seating capacities of any NHL arena.

fter Anaheim knocked the Flames out of the
006 playoffs, the general manager of the
ucks said, "The city of Calgary has one of
e best hockey cultures in the League, thanks
the class and passion the fans provide in
e Saddledome... The Saddledome is one
ugh building to play in, due to the fans and
e Sea of Red."

he Saddledome is also home to the Calgary
oughnecks of the National Lacrosse League
nd the Calgary Hitmen of the Western
ockey League (WHL), a hockey league for
nior teams. Players are drafted from the
HL to the NHL through the Entry Draft.

**The Hitmen are owned and operated by the
Calgary Flames.**

About the Mascot

Harvey the Hound has been the Flames
mascot since 1983. He was the first NHL
mascot. Harvey is huge. He is 6-feet-6-
inches tall and weighs 200 pounds. He
entertains fans and leads cheers to draw
the crowd into the spirit of the game.

Sometimes he distracts opposing teams
with his antics. Once, the Oilers' coach
ripped out Harvey's big, cloth tongue.
Harvey had been taunting him from
behind the bench.

Hockey Positions

The positions in hockey are forward, defence, and goaltender. Each team is allowed six players on the ice. Teams usually play with three forwards, two defencemen, and one goaltender. The forwards include a right winger, left winger, and centre. The defensive pair is a right defender and a left defender.

The main job of all three forwards is to pass the puck up the ice and score goals. The centre generally takes the **face-off**. The right winger usually stays along the boards on the right side of the rink. The left winger does the same along the left side.

The centre generally plays between the two wingers and follows the puck.

Theoren Fleury, Lanny McDonald, and Kent Nilsson were all successful forwards with the Flames. Fleury collected 830 points during the time he played with the Flames—the most ever achieved by any player on the team. McDonald scored the most goals in a season with 66, and Nilsson gained the most points at 131.

It is the defencemen's job to prevent the opposition from scoring goals. They do this by staying between their goalie and the opposing players. They also force the opposition players out of good shooting position whenever possible. Some defenders also score goals and create scoring chances for their forwards. This type of defender is called an offensive defenceman. Al MacInnis was a defenceman who scored 213 goals and had 609 assists as a Flame.

FLAMES ALL-TIME LEADERS

Most Goals
Theoren Fleury
364 goals

Most Assists
Al MacInnis
609 assists

Most Points
Theoren Fleury
830 points

Most Games Played
Al MacInnis 803 games

Most Seasons Played
Al MacInnis and Theoren Fleury, 11 seasons each for the Calgary Flames

Most Penalty Minutes
Tim Hunter
2,405 **penalty** minutes

Most Goaltender Wins
Mike Vernon
259 wins

he other type of defender is a stay-at-home
efenceman, such as Rhett Warrener. Stay-at-
ome defencemen rarely race up ice with the
uck. Instead, they generally stay close to
eir goalie to help prevent the other team
om scoring.

he goalie's job is to stop the puck from going
 the net. Goalies are the last line of defence.
 they miss the puck, a goal is scored. Mike
ernon played goal in Calgary for many years.
e was the goalie who helped the Flames win
he Stanley Cup in 1989. He won a total of 259
ames as a Flame, and 39 games in one season.
he first year Miikka Kiprusoff played for the
ames, he had the lowest goals against average
 the league at 1.69. He is known for staying
ool under pressure.

**Mike Vernon was the Flames' top goalie
between the 1986–1987 and 1993–1994 seasons.**

The Goalie and his mask

Goalies express themselves through special designs on their masks. Miikka Kiprusoff has "Kipper" painted across the bottom of his mask. Kipper is his nickname. On the rest of his mask are fiery flames. These flames represent his pride in playing for the Flames.

Roman Turek, the 6-foot-4-inch tall goaltender from the Czech Republic, played for the Flames from 2001 to 2004. His masks featured his favourite band—Iron Maiden. When in Calgary, he had "Eddie," the band's mascot, painted on his mask. All of Turek's masks during his nine-year NHL career featured this band in some form.

Mike Vernon's mask from the 1980s is in the Hockey Hall of Fame in Toronto. This mask features a series of flames flowing from the front of the mask to the back. A later version had the fire-breathing horse from the Flame's third jersey painted on the front. It also had larger flames shooting down the sides.

Hockey Equipment

Hockey is a fast, rough sport. Players wear padded equipment to prevent injuries. Hockey equipment is like body armor. It includes helmets, padded gloves, knee-length padded pants, and loose stretchy jerseys. They also wear shoulder pads, elbow pads, and thick socks with shin pads underneath. Some players, such as Jarome Iginla and Dion Phaneuf, wear a visor on their helmet to protect their eyes. Tony Amonte, a Flames **veteran** forward, does not wear a protective visor. Most players entering the league today wear visors.

Today's skates are made of leather and various plastic materials. Skates are designed for speed. Players have their skate blades sharpened many times throughout the season.

Goalies wear special equipment for protection from hard shots fired at them. Some players can fire the puck faster than 150 kilometres per hour. In fact, Al MacInnis, a former Flame, has won the NHL All Star "hardest shot" skills competition seven times. In 2003, his shot was clocked at 159.2 kilometres per hour.

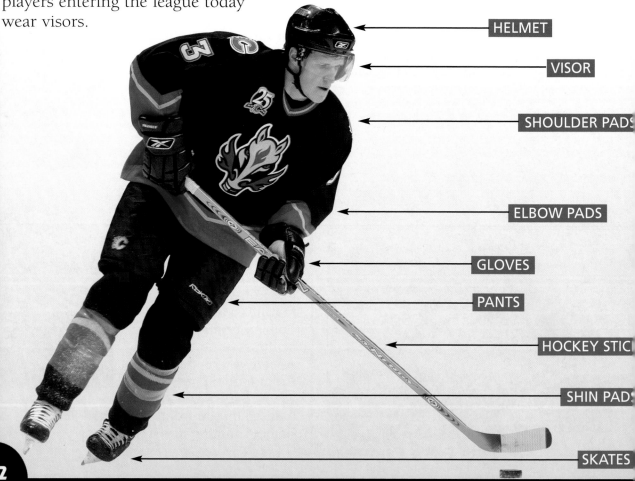

HELMET

VISOR

SHOULDER PADS

ELBOW PADS

GLOVES

PANTS

HOCKEY STICK

SHIN PADS

SKATES

12

altenders wear thick pads that reach from
eir thighs to their skates. They use these
ds to kick or deflect the puck away from
e net. They also wear a catcher or trapper
one hand and a blocker on the other. A
alie's catcher is similar to a baseball glove.
e blocker is a glove attached to a long, flat,
dded surface. Goalies use the blocker to
flect the puck into the corner, away from
e net.

Team Jerseys

In the past, all hockey games were played on outdoor rinks. Players wore turtleneck sweaters and knitted wool caps to keep warm. Today, teams wear matching jerseys bearing their team logo.

The Calgary Flames wear three different jerseys. Their home jersey is red with a fiery C. Their road jersey is white with a fiery C. Their third jersey is the "Year of the Cowboy" jersey. It features the head of a horse with flames coming out of its nostrils. It represents "horse power with attitude." This jersey is only worn occasionally during the season.

From time to time, teams change the look of their jerseys. In 2004, the Flames introduced a new, red-hot jersey with a fiery C.

Fans wear red jerseys to games during the playoffs. Then, the Saddledome becomes a "Sea of Red."

GOALIE MASK

OALIE STICK

GOALIE PADS

CATCHER

BLOCKER

13

Competing in the National Hockey League

There are currently 30 teams in the National Hockey League. Half of the teams play in the Eastern Conference. The other half play in the Western Conference. Each conference is made up of three divisions. In the Eastern Conference, the divisions include the Atlantic Division, the Northeast Division, and the Southeast Division, while in the Western Conference, the Central Division, the Northwest Division, and the Pacific Division are included.

Eight teams from each conference advance from the regular season to the playoffs. Playoff spots in the conference quarter finals are awarded on the basis of points earned during the regular season. Teams are **seeded** from #1 to 8 based on their regular-season points. Four series are then played with #1 playing #8, #2 playing #7, and so on. Each series is a best-of-seven format. The first team to win four games wins the series.

Winners of the conference quarter finals advance to the conference semifinals. The winning teams are then seeded in each series, based on the same criteria as the quarter finals. Winners of the semifinal series then advance to the conference finals. Conference winners play each other for the Stanley Cup.

The Flames won the Stanley Cup in 1989.

WESTERN CONFERENCE

Central Division	Northwest Division	Pacific Division
CHICAGO BLACKHAWKS	CALGARY FLAMES	ANAHEIM DUCKS
COLUMBUS BLUE JACKETS	COLORADO AVALANCHE	DALLAS STARS
DETROIT RED WINGS	EDMONTON OILERS	LOS ANGELES KINGS
NASHVILLE PREDATORS	MINNESOTA WILD	PHOENIX COYOTES
ST. LOUIS BLUES	VANCOUVER CANUCKS	SAN JOSE SHARKS

WESTERN CONFERENCE

| #1 versus #8 | #2 versus #7 |
| #3 versus #6 | #4 versus #5 |

QUARTER FINALS

Top four teams move to next round

| #1 versus #4 |
| #2 versus #3 |

SEMIFINALS

Top two teams move to next round

| #1 versus #2 |

CONFERENCE FINALS

Top team moves to last round

EASTERN CONFERENCE

| #1 versus #8 | #2 versus #7 |
| #3 versus #6 | #4 versus #5 |

Top four teams move to next round

| #1 versus #4 |
| #2 versus #3 |

Top two teams move to next round

| #1 versus #2 |

Top team moves to last round

Top in West → Versus ← Top in East

Stanley Cup Champion

EASTERN CONFERENCE

Atlantic Division	**Northeast Division**	**Southeast Division**
NEW JERSEY DEVILS	BOSTON BRUINS	ATLANTA THRASHERS
NEW YORK ISLANDERS	BUFFALO SABRES	CAROLINA HURRICANES
NEW YORK RANGERS	MONTREAL CANADIENS	FLORIDA PANTHERS
PHILADELPHIA FLYERS	OTTAWA SENATORS	TAMPA BAY LIGHTNING
PITTSBURGH PENGUINS	TORONTO MAPLE LEAFS	WASHINGTON CAPITALS

15

The Battle of Alberta

Calgary and Edmonton have been battling each other for bragging rights in sports since before Alberta became a province in 1905. The first hockey battle between the two cities was between the Calgary All-Stars and the Edmonton Thistles in 1898. They were the two best hockey teams in Alberta at that time.

Since then the Battle of Alberta, between the Calgary Flames and the Edmonton Oilers, has become one of the biggest **rivalries** in the history of Canadian sports.

The Flames and the Oilers are both in the Northwest Division of the Western Conference. They play each other many times during the regular season. They often face each other in the playoffs. This causes rivalries to develop between individual players. Some individual battles can last for years. When these teams play each other, the atmosphere in the arena is electric. Fans expect an intense game.

In the 1980s, the Oilers were a dominant force in the NHL. The Battle of Alberta

came one-sided during that decade. The
ilers won the Stanley Cup in 1984, 1985,
987, 1988, and 1990. The Flames won the
up in 1989.

1986, the Flames defeated the Oilers
the playoffs. It was the first time they had
efeated the Oilers in a playoff series. This
as as good as a Stanley Cup victory in the
inds of many Flames fans. They had finally
onquered their biggest rivals.

The Battle of the Fans

Most Calgary fans are from Calgary and
southern Alberta. Most Oilers fans are from
Edmonton and northern Alberta. Radio
stations, newspapers, and fans across the
province gloat whenever their team wins.

Bragging rights are always at stake
whenever Calgary and Edmonton compete.
There is much good-natured ribbing before
and after hockey games when the Flames
and Oilers play each other.

Making It to the NHL

Each year in June, the National Hockey League has a draft. It is called the NHL Entry Draft. During the Entry Draft, NHL teams select players from the Canadian Hockey League (CHL) and various **semi-professional** leagues around the world to play on their team. Teams that finish low in the NHL regular-season standings select first. Teams that finish high in the standings select last. This order helps balance the talent pool in the league. Many players that are drafted have played in the Canadian Hockey League.

The CHL is a junior league made up of players that are 16 to 20 years of age. Sometimes drafted players are returned to the CHL to further develop their skills. Chuck Kobasew of the Flames was drafted in the fir round in 2001. He spent the next season developing his skills with the Kelowna Rockets of the CHL before playing his first game with the Flames in 2002–03.

Some hockey players never play for the NHL teams that draft them. Jarome Iginla was drafted by the Dallas Stars in the first round in 1995, but he never played a game with them.

◾ **Dion Phaneuf was selected ninth overall by the Calgary Flames in the 2003 NHL Entry Draft.**

...inla was acquired by the Flames in a trade ...fore he played his first NHL game. Teams ...en trade players for players. They also trade ...ayers for draft choices.

...HL team **rosters** are made up of signed ...ayers. NHL teams sign the players that they ...ink will give them the best chance of ...inning. Tony Amonte was signed by the ...ames in 2005.

...gned players may be sent to the American ...ockey League (AHL) for a while. The AHL is ...semi-professional league. All NHL franchises ...wn an AHL team. Players that are too old to ...ay in the CHL are often sent to the AHL to ...evelop their skills. Some players play for ...ars in the AHL before having an opportunity ...o play in the NHL. Matthew Lombardi of the ...ames played 76 games with the Saint John ...ames before he joined the Calgary Flames. ...he Saint John Flames was Calgary's AHL ...am at that time. Now, Calgary's AHL team ...s the Omaha Ak-Sar-Ben Knights.

Matthew Lombardi was the Flames' third-round draft choice in the 2002 NHL Entry Draft.

Reporting on the Flames

**Reporting on the Flames
Ed Whalen, Calgary Legend and
Flames Beloved Broadcaster**

Ed Whalen was the Flames' legendary broadcaster in the 1980s and early 90s. He was also the host of Stampede Wrestling in Calgary. Ed Whalen was a popular member of the Calgary sports community. He was known for his interesting broadcasting expressions, such as "That was a ring-a-ding-dong dandy affair."

A city arena and the broadcasting studio at the Saddledome have been named after Whalen, who died in 2001.

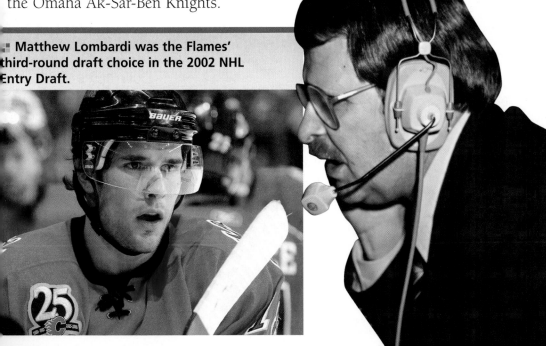

The Olympics

Canadian Olympic Men's Hockey

The Canadian Olympic Men's hockey team is made up of the best hockey players of Canadian citizenship. NHL hockey fans from across the country cheer for them in the Olympics. The Canadian team's main rivals are Russia, the United States, the Czech Republic, Finland, and Sweden. Since 1920, Canada has won seven gold medals in Olympic hockey.

In the past, NHL players were not able to compete in the Winter Olympics. Canada would send amateur players to the games. In 1998, NHL players began to play on Canada Olympic hockey team. Canada failed to capture a medal that year in Nagano, Japan. This was very disappointing for the team and for hockey fans across Canada. In 2002, Team Canada captured the gold medal in Salt Lake City, Utah. They defeated the United States in the gold medal game. Hockey fans from across Canada were delighted by the victory. Flames star, Jarome Iginla, was a big part of the team's success. He scored four points in the tournament and played on the team's number one line with Joe Sakic and Mario Lemieux.

In six games at the 2002 Olympics, Jarome Iginla scored three goals and one assist.

FLAMES PARTICIPATION ON TEAM CANADA
2006 Winter Olympics in Turin, Italy   Jarome Iginla   Robyn Regehr
2002 Winter Olympics in Salt Lake City, Utah   Jarome Iginla
1998 Winter Olympics in Nagano, Japan   Theoren Fleury
1988 Winter Olympics in Calgary, Alberta   Jim Peplinski

Canadian Olympic Women's Hockey

The Canadian Olympic Women's hockey team began competing in the Winter Olympics in 1998. Their team is made up of players from the National Women's Hockey League. The Canadian women's team's biggest international rival is the United States. In 1998, Canada lost to the United States in the gold medal game. Hockey fans in Canada were devastated. However, Canada beat the U.S. team in the gold medal round in 2002 in Salt Lake City, Utah. Then, in 2006, they beat Sweden in Turin, Italy, to again capture the gold medal. The team is led by star forwards Cassie Campbell and Hayley Wickenheiser. Wickenheiser is the only woman to ever score a goal in a professional men's hockey league game. The Canadian Olympic Women's team trains at the Olympic Oval in Calgary. This is because the Olympic Oval has an international-sized rink.

The Canadian Olympic Women's hockey team outscored their opponents 28–0 in their first two round robin games of the 2006 Olympics in Turin, Italy.

21

Popular Flames Coache

Al MacNeil

The first coach of the Calgary Flames was Al MacNeil. He coached the Flames the last year they were in Atlanta and guided them through their first season in Calgary. He coached the team again for part of the 2002–03 season. MacNeil was an NHL player in the 1950s and 60s. He played 524 regular-season games with the Toronto Maple Leafs, the Montreal Canadiens, the Chicago Blackhawks, the New York Rangers, and the Pittsburgh Penguins. In 1971, MacNeil became head coach of the Canadiens. That year, they won the Stanley Cup.

Bob Johnson

Before moving to Calgary, Bob Johnson was head coach of the Badgers hockey team at the University of Wisconsin. He led the Badgers to seven college championship tournaments and won three of them. During this time, he earned the nickname "Badger Bob." Johnson began coaching the Calgary Flames in 1982 and coached them for 5 years. Badger Bob led the Flames to th Stanley Cup finals in 1986, but then lost to the Montreal Canadiens. He was well-known for his positive attitude. His most famous phrase was "It's a great day for hockey!" Afte his years in Calgary, he became executive director of USA Hockey. Then he returned to the NHL to coach the Pittsburgh Penguin

Terry Crisp

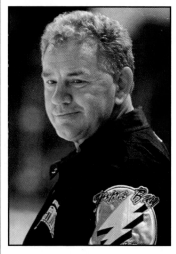

Terry Crisp's nickname is "Crispy." He was born in 1943 in Parry Sound, Ontario. Crisp played in 536 regular-season games in the NHL He won the Stanley Cup with the Philadelphia Flyers in 1974 and 1975. Crisp began his coaching career in 1977 as an assistant coac with the Flyers. He joined the Calgary Flame as their head coach in 1987. Two years later, he guided the team to a Stanley Cup victory. He was so delighted with the win that he climbed over the glass behind the bench and kissed one of the fans. Later, Crisp became a hockey broadcaster for the Nashville Predators.

Darryl Sutter

The Sutter family is one of the best-known families to ever play in the NHL. Together, the six brothers played in more than 5,000 NHL games. Darryl Sutter played for the Chicago Blackhawks from 1979 to 1987. He scored 279 points in eight NHL seasons. In 1985, he scored 12 goals in the playoffs. This is a Chicago Blackhawks playoff record. He also set the record for most overtime goals in a single playoff series. Sutter scored two overtime goals against the Minnesota North Stars in 1985. His coaching career began in Chicago in 1987. In 1992, Sutter guided the Blackhawks to the Stanley Cup finals. Sutter became the head coach of the Calgary Flames in 2002. The following year, he guided the Flames to the Stanley Cup finals.

Making the Call

As well as coaches and players, the NHL needs game officials. Game officials are linesmen and referees. Linesmen call **offsides** and **icing**, while referees call most of the penalties. Referees need to be good skaters because they have to keep up with the play for an entire game. Unlike hockey players, referees are not able to rest between **shifts**.

Referees are so important to hockey that several referees have been inducted into the Hockey Hall of Fame. You can read about them on the Hockey Hall of Fame website at *www.legendsofhockey.net*.

The first step to becoming a referee is to contact a local league office. Training is available at officiating schools, such as the North American School of Officiating in Guelph, Ontario. These schools teach ice positioning, signals, penalty calling, skating skills, and off-ice theory.

A referee needs all of these skills so that he or she can make the right calls during a game. Every year, referees attend a week-long training camp. During the camp, fitness level and skating ability are tested. At the end of the week, referees leave camp and head to their first game of the season.

Unforgettable Moments

In 1986, the Flames defeated the Oilers in the second round of the playoffs. This was the first time that they had ever defeated Edmonton in the playoffs. Steve Smith, an Oilers defenceman, accidentally scored on his own net. This goal made the difference in the outcome of the game. Flames fans were delighted. They had finally defeated their biggest rivals. For some Flames fans, this victory was as good as winning the Stanley Cup.

That year, the Flames advanced to the Stanley Cup finals. They played the Montreal Canadiens. This was the first time in 10 years that two Canadian teams competed for the Stanley Cup, and the first time the Flames had ever made it to the Stanley Cup finals. The Flames lost to the Canadiens. However, the Flames did establish themselves as one of the **premier** teams in the league.

In 1989, the Flames captured the Stanley Cup in six games. They conquered the Canadiens in the Montreal Forum. The Flames were the first opposition team ever to win the Stanley Cup in this legendary building.

In the 1989 Stanley Cup playoffs, Joe Mullen led the Calgary Flames in scoring, with 16 goals in 21 games.

2004, the Flames made it back to the nley Cup finals. This was very special ause they had missed the playoffs the vious seven seasons. Few people in the key world thought that they would make hat far. They had only finished as the sixth d in their conference that year. On their y to the finals, they defeated the number one seeded Detroit Red Wings, the number two seeded San Jose Sharks, and the number three seeded Vancouver Canucks. Fans were delighted. Although the Flames lost in the finals to the Tampa Bay Lightning, they won the hearts of hockey fans across Canada.

NHL INDIVIDUAL AND TEAM AWARDS WON BY THE FLAMES

Name of Award	Awarded to	Flames Winners
t Ross Trophy	the player with the most points during the regular season	Jarome Iginla, 2001–02
ster B. Pearson Award	the player voted by his fellow NHL players as the most valuable player in the league	Jarome Iginla, 2001–02
aurice "Rocket" chard Trophy	the player who scores the most goals in the regular season	Jarome Iginla, 2001–02 Jarome Iginla, co-winner in 2003–04
onn Smythe Trophy	the most valuable player during the playoffs	Al MacInnis, 1988–89
lder Trophy	the best rookie, or first-year player	Gary Suter, 1985–86 Joe Nieuwendyk, 1987–88 Sergei Makarov, 1989–90
dy Byng Trophy	the player who best combines hockey skill, sportsmanship, and gentlemanly conduct	Joe Mullen, 1986–87 Joe Mullen, 1988–89
esident's Trophy	the best team during the regular season	Calgary Flames, 1987–88 Calgary Flames, 1988–89

Flames Legends and Current Stars

#9 Lanny McDonald

CAREER FACTS

Lanny McDonald was traded to the Flames in 1981 and played eight seasons for them. He retired in 1989, after the Flames won the Stanley Cup. He was known for his great shot, his skating ability, and his toughness. He was also known for his big, bushy, red mustache. He became one of the best scorers in the NHL. He recorded 500 goals and 506 assists in 1,111 regular-season NHL games. Few players in the history of the NHL have scored more than 500 goals.

Position Forward
Born February 16, 1953

Hometown
Hanna, Alberta

#39 Doug Gilmour

CAREER FACTS

In 1,474 regular-season NHL games, Doug Gilmour recorded 450 goals and 964 assists. In 1987, he played for Team Canada in the **Canada Cup**. He was named the most valuable player in this tournament. He was traded from the St. Louis Blues to the Calgary Flames in 1988. He won the Stanley Cup with the Flames in 1989. Doug later became part of one of the biggest hockey trades in NHL history. In 1990–91, the Flames traded him to the Toronto Maple Leafs as part of a 10-player deal.

Position Centre
Born June 25, 1963

Hometown
Kingston, Ontario

#12 Jarome Iginla

CAREER FACTS

Jarome Iginla is the captain of the Calgary Flames. He has never played for any other NHL team. Iginla is known as a **power forward**. He is good at hitting and scoring goals. In 2001–02, he won the Maurice "Rocket" Richard Trophy as the league's top goal scorer. He also won the Art Ross Trophy, with 96 points, the most in the NHL that year. In 2003–04, Jarome won the Maurice "Rocket" Richard Trophy for the second time.

Position Right Wing
Born July 1, 1977

Hometown
Edmonton, Alberta

Darryl Sutter said this about Jarome Iginla: "In my 25 years in hockey, that was the single most dominant game I've ever seen a player play."

#34 Miikka Kiprusoff

CAREER FACTS

Miikka Kiprusoff began his NHL career with the San Jose Sharks. He was traded to Calgary in 2003. Since then, many people think he has become one of the best goalies in the NHL. His fine play helped the Flames advance to the Stanley Cup finals in 2004. Miikka set a new Flames record in the 2005–06 regular season by winning 42 games. He also recorded 10 shutouts during that time.

Position Goaltender
Born October 26, 1976

Hometown
Turco, Finland

Craig Conroy of the Flames said this about Miikka Kiprusoff: "Kipper gave us a chance. We have a whole different kind of confidence with him back there."

The Best Years

At the end of Lanny McDonald's last NHL game, he embraced the Stanley Cup. Three years later, in 1992, he was elected to the Hockey Hall of Fame.

In 1985–86, the Flames finished second in their conference behind the Edmonton Oilers, and sixth in the overall standings. The team was improving. Player trades, such as Lanny McDonald from the Colorado Rockies, made the team stronger. As well, rookie defenceman Gary Suter had a terrific season. He captured the Calder Trophy as the best rookie in the NHL.

During the playoffs, the Flames swept the Winnipeg Jets in three straight games. The the Flames and Oilers alternated wins with the Flames pulling off an upset victory in the seventh game. This was the first playoff series win for the Flames over the Oilers. Then the Flames played the St. Louis Blues, before meeting the Montreal Canadiens in the final. This was the first all-Canadian Stanley Cup Final since the NHL expansion in 1967. The Flames won Game 1. However, the Canadiens rallied to win the next four games.

For several years after, the Flames continued to be one of the NHL's top teams in the regular season. I the playoffs, they were not as successful. However, in 1989, the

n the President's Trophy for the second
aight year. The Flames were tested
ly in the playoffs when they were
shed to a seventh game by the
ncouver Canucks. In the next
ries, the Flames swept the Los
geles Kings in four straight
mes and the Chicago Blackhawks
five games. In the finals, the
mes faced the Montreal Canadiens.
Game 6, they won the cup. The
mes became the first road team to ever
n the cup at the Forum. Defenceman Al
cInnis won the Conn Smythe Trophy as
st Valuable Player (MVP) of the playoffs.
nny McDonald finally embraced the Stanley
p after 18 years in the NHL. That was
nny's last NHL game.

e Flames had a good season in 2003–04,
th 94 points. They finished sixth in the
nference and twelfth in the overall
ndings. What made this season special,
wever, was that they advanced to the
nley Cup Finals. Nobody predicted that the
mes would have so much success in the
yoffs. They surprised themselves and
ers with their gritty performance.
wever, they lost to the Tampa Bay
ghtning in the seventh game of the
als. Even though they lost, it was
memorable season.

FLAMES IN THE COMMUNITY

The Calgary Flames also contribute to the community off the ice. They help Calgarians by being involved in charities and other helpful organizations. The Flames Foundation for Life has given millions of dollars to education, medical research, health, and amateur sports.

Robin Regehr is the official spokesperson for The Party Program. This program teaches young people about the risks of drinking alcohol. Jarome Iginla is involved with a program called KidSport. This program provides sporting equipment to children whose families cannot afford to buy it themselves. Iginla is also involved with the Juvenile Diabetes Research Foundation. He participates in many events to help raise money for this cause. These events include annual golf tournaments and the Walk to Cure Diabetes.

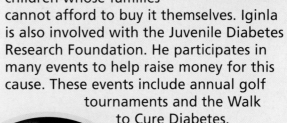

The Flames House is another valuable contribution the Flames are making to the community. The Flames House will be southern Alberta's first free **hospice** for sick children. The Flames hope to open the doors to the hospice in 2007.

Quiz

1 Where and when was the first hockey game played?

2 How many teams play in the NHL today?

3 Where did the Flames franchise begin?

4 What was the name of the Flames' first home arena?

5 What is the name of the Flames' current home arena in Calgary?

6 Which former Flames player sports a bushy, red mustache?

7 What year did the Flames win their only Stanley Cup?

8 Who did the Flames defeat to capture the Stanley Cup?

9 Which Calgary Flame led the league in goals in 2001–02?

10 Who was the first Calgary Flames coach?

Answers

The first hockey game was played at the Victoria Skating [rin]k in Montreal in 1875.

There are 30 teams in the [N]HL today.

The Flames franchise began [in] Atlanta, Georgia.

The Flames' first home arena [w]as called the Omni.

The Flames' home arena [in] Calgary is called the [Pe]ngrowth Saddledome.

Lanny McDonald wore a [bu]shy, red moustache.

The Flames won their only [St]anley Cup in 1989.

The Flames defeated the [M]ontreal Canadiens.

Jarome Iginla led the league [in] goals.

[10]. Al MacNeil was the first [C]algary Flames coach.

30

Further Research

any books and websites provide information on the Flames. To learn more about the
ames, borrow books from the library, or surf the Internet.

— BOOKS TO READ —

libraries have computers that connect to a database for researching information. If
nput a key word, you will be provided with a list of books in the library that contain
nation on that topic. Non-fiction books are arranged numerically, using their call number.
n books are organized alphabetically by the author's last name.

— ONLINE SITES —

rn more about the Calgary Flames, type in key words such as "Calgary Flames"
HL teams" into the search field.

www.calgaryflames.com

www.flamesfans.com

www. pengrowthsaddledome.com

Glossary

amateur: a player who is not a professional and plays a sport for the pleasure of it without being paid money to play

Canada Cup: a hockey tournament featuring the best players in the world representing their countries

Civil War: the war from 1861 to 1865 between the northern and southern states

entry draft: a process used by NHL teams to select new players

face-off: when the referee drops the puck between two players to start the play

franchises: teams or organizations that become members of a league

funds: money set aside for hockey expenses

Great Depression: the time between 1929 and 1934 when business was bad and many people lost their jobs

Hockey Hall of Fame: a place where former players and people involved in hockey are honored for their contributions to the game

hospice: a home for people that are ill or destitute

icing: a stoppage in play caused by a player shooting the puck from his or her side of the centre line to the opposition's goal line without it being touched

offsides: stoppages in play caused by a player crossing the offensive blue line before the puck

opposition: a team that opposes another team

penalty: a punishment for breaking a rule of the game

playoff: a final game or series of games played to decide who will be champion

power forward: a forward who combines skill and toughness

premier: first in importance or position

professional: a person who earns a living from a sport

rivalries: two teams competing against each other to be better than the other

rosters: lists of players playing on a team

seeded: being placed in a specific rank or position

semi-professional: a player who plays for money, but is paid less than what professionals are paid

shifts: periods of time when a player is on the ice during a game

Stanley Cup: the National Hockey League's prize for the best team in the playoffs

veteran: a player who has considerable experience playing in the NHL

Index